MW01247143

WHAT PEOPLE ARE SAYING

"It was a pleasure to work with Mike Lee."
— Stephen Curry, NBA MVP

"Mike Lee approaches success and performance from a coach's perspective, understanding that to be a top 'athlete' in any industry requires optimizing one's performance in 4 different domains: mind, body, spirit, and emotions. Mike's latest book is a manual for individual and organizational high performance, combining his many years of coaching experience and research into evidence-based practices. The practical, hands-on exercises and compelling stories of their application produce a visionary guide on how to get better at just about anything-including engagement, retention, talent attraction, and transformational leadership. And, you'll find purpose and fulfillment doing it."
— Eric Severson, Chief People and Belonging Officer, Neiman Marcus Group

"I've had the opportunity to experience Mike both virtually and live, in-person. Regardless of how you decide to work with him, you're going to walk away with strategies to better navigate through adversity, build focus and enhance overall professional performance. His content, stories, and mindsets could not be more relevant at this time!"

— **Brad Pavelec,** Cisco

"Mike's message is inspiring and message rooted in practicality. The strategies he's teaching will help your people unlock the potential within."

— **Larry Murphy,** Chief Strategy Officer, The Walt Disney Company

"If you're looking to inspire and elevate your people, look no further. Mike helped our leaders really focus on purpose-driven, heartfelt leadership that will have a huge impact on our culture of belonging and well being. His new book will help you with the same."

— **Rich Steffen,** President, American Family Insurance

"*Leadership is a lifelong game fueled by daily growth, humility, confidence, courage, and the ability to ground yourself with a beginners mindset—because leadership never stops. In order to keep up with this frenetic pace, we need a playbook to show us the way of the future. Thanks to Mike Lee, the future is in your hands.*"

— **Paul Epstein,** Former NBA and NFL Executive, Keynote Speaker

"*For decades business leaders have leveraged the sports world to adopt best practices in high-performance, leadership, and culture. The parallels between the two worlds are endless. Mike's new book applies the same philosophies to help leaders and organizations win in the new world of work.*"

— **Alan Stein Jr.,** Author of Raise Your Game, Keynote Speaker

"*Leaders have to evolve to stay relevant without losing their authenticity. This book provides timely and actionable insights on how leaders can prepare themselves and their business for the future.*"

— **Chris Drees,** President and CEO, Menasha Corporation

"Mike was literally the perfect choice to kick off our event and set the tone for the rest of the day with Jesse Itzler and Mike Tyson. The basketball stories had takeaways for a general audience even if you don't follow the game and left everyone wanting more. I couldn't believe how fast the hour went by! We would have him back in a heartbeat!"

— **Chris Flakus,** CEO, CSI Companies

"If you want someone who understands the power of presence, performance, and people then Mike Lee is your go-to person. Every encounter we have exchanged left me a wiser and bolder leader and human being. Mike knows the theory, the practice, and how to deliver them. What else do you need if you are looking to build presence, resiliency, leadership, and peak performance."

— **Patrick Kozakiewicz,** Global Mindfulness Program Leader, IBM

"Mike's message on the power of the present moment was incredibly impactful. He spent time up front getting to understand our business, people and industry and was able to seamlessly tie his talk into our North America Annual Meeting theme. Mike brought a unique combination of energy and compassion that really connected with our people. And, I know his message not only impacted our people's lives, but will support us in reaching our strategic initiatives."

— **James Rooney,** CEO and Chairman, DazPak

"Listening to and learning from Mike has not only been a positive experience but also a powerful one. In a world of change, he has a knack for simple tools that help you focus on a path forward. It's been great to connect with him over the past year, both one-on-one and in larger groups — he's able to keep everyone engaged and it will be great to see him in person one day soon."

— **Richard Curtis,** CEO, FutureBrand Australia

"As a veteran producer and educator in the meetings and events space, I can say without hesitation that Mike is the easiest, most empathetic, and most conscientious speaker I've ever worked with. From our first pre-event call to our post-event debrief, it was clear Mike was invested in our meeting goals, customizing his message to help us best fulfill them, and then following up to ensure he had. On stage, he's as authentic and accessible as he is off, personifying the heart-centered, mindful leadership approach he talks about so passionately. A talk, by the way, that at this particular time, is very relevant, and exactly what executives need to hear to lead contemporary (and future) workforces."

— **Anthony Bollotta,** Executive Producer, Bollotta Entertainment

"I love the storytelling!"

— **IBM**

"I appreciated your authenticity, your vulnerability, and your humbleness. Your sharing of personal examples brought many of the concepts alive."

— **John Graham,** Chief Marketing Officer, Dutch Bros Coffee

"Your stories, strategies and exercises were timely for where we are at right now and where we want to go. We loved that you sat in on earlier sessions and were able to create call backs in your talk from our COO's keynote. The theatric walk-on video, music during the interactive exercises and your presentation style kept the energy up even at the end of a long day."

— **Avetta**

NEW RULES
FOR THE
FUTURE OF
LEADERSHIP

NEW RULES
FOR THE
FUTURE OF
LEADERSHIP

How the bold and driven can elevate
engagement, win the war for talent,
and create a culture of belonging

MIKE LEE

Published by HeartMind Press

Mike Lee
MindShift Labs
LOS ANGELES, CA

Copyright © 2023 by Mike Lee

ISBN: 9798211689367

*"To the bold and driven looking to elevate
their influence and impact by leading with love."*

Contents

"
We can't predict the future. But we can prepare for it by mastering the internal game. When the future is here it's too late to prepare."

— Mike Lee

Introduction
A NEW WORLD

In early 2020 when the whole world shut down, I think all of us were trying to find things we could do to find a sense of normalcy. In the first forty-five days of lockdown in Los Angeles, I saw no one except for my neighbor and the people at the grocery store. Besides the loneliness of the virtual-only work environment, the gyms, beaches, and parks were closed. As someone who was leading a small business and building another one on the side, I am very intentional about setting my mental and emotional state for the day. I know that only when I'm the best version of myself will I be able to show up for others. Before the lockdown, I started every morning with HIIT training, a spin class, or a yoga class to set the tone for my day, which would lead to my morning routine. So one way that I found some structure was by getting outside for runs. It was something that I could do to help me find a sense of routine and be grounded with the overwhelming stress of my entire calendar wiped clean. By June, I had developed some typical routes I would run in my neighborhood. But one early evening, I went out for a run, and the route was nothing but typical.

I had my APL running shoes tied up, my AirPods in, and my Deep House playlist loaded on Spotify—but those were the only things that were the same.

We have jasmine flowers throughout my neighborhood, which were blooming at the time. The scent of these flowers was replaced by the smell of sawdust. The construction I usually heard from the apartment next door was replaced by the sound of stores being boarded up just a block away.

As I ran further, I arrived at the intersection of La Cienega and Beverly Boulevard. This is usually one of the busiest intersections in Los Angeles, where tons of people wait to cross the street to go into a shopping center.

This intersection was empty. The National Guard replaced these people with armored vehicles and assault rifles, activated due to the protests and rioting. It was only about ten minutes before our 6 pm curfew, so I turned the corner and headed back to my building.

As I finished the last couple of blocks of my run, I kept saying to myself, "This is insane. What is happening right now is insane. How am I going to lead myself through this unprecedented uncertainty? And how will I help people who rely on me for guidance?" It was this surreal moment where I saw all these things colliding: the global pandemic, a digital first work environment, the social justice movement, and the uncertainty.

While I was stretching on the stairs outside of my apartment, I had a few realizations:

1. Leaders have never had to deal with more things at once. One of these challenges would have been tough, but all of them happening simultaneously is unprecedented. And senior leaders, emerging leaders, and leaders without a title need to be equipped with internal skills to navigate this new world of work long after the pandemic.

2. The world we once knew is gone forever. COVID-19 has changed everything. While it was disruptive initially, it is also an incredible opportunity for those who take advantage.

3. The old leadership paradigm is broken. Instead of a sole focus on shareholder profits and KPI's, leaders today are being challenged to use their businesses as a vehicle for social impact, well-being, purpose and belonging. And, people are increasingly expecting the companies they work for, and spend their money with, to be a force for good — both for them as employees, and for the world. If leaders continue to follow the old leadership paradigm they'll lose themselves, lose their people and lose their stakeholders.

While I'd never been through a pandemic, my life and work experience in many ways had prepared me to meet the moment. Leading myself and others through change was incredibly familiar to me — including my own internal paradigm shift. I was no stranger to adversity. And I knew that many of the answers were already within.

Fast forward to today, and companies are dealing with five major challenges:

THE PURPOSE CRISIS

Mckinsey found that nearly two-thirds of US-based employees surveyed said that COVID-19 caused them to reflect on their purpose in life. And nearly half said that they are reconsidering the kind of work they do because of the pandemic.[1] Leaders can no longer ignore this, especially when managing Gen Z and Millennials.

THE ENGAGEMENT DILEMMA

Second, companies are working harder than ever to retain and engage their existing population of employees. Global employee engagement is at an all time low costing companies $7.8 trillion annually.[2]

THE WAR FOR TALENT

Companies are also fighting for a smaller and smaller pool of qualified talent. COVID-19 changed what current employees and job seekers need, expect, and want from their work experience and those that lead them.

Companies and leaders need to create a work experience their people can't wait to talk about.

This starts with the human connection that makes people feel like they belong to something bigger than themselves.

OUTDATED AND DYSFUNCTIONAL LEADERSHIP STYLES

And lastly, mountains of research show senior and emerging leaders are not equipped with the skills for the future. Business schools traditionally cover skills like strategy and are missing out on the heart-centered leadership skills that research shows are increasingly important. A Forbes article argued that empathy is the number one leadership skill required in today's world of work.[3] According to a recent Fortune survey, only 7 percent of CEOs believe their companies are building effective global leaders, and just 10 percent said that their leadership development initiatives have a clear business impact.[4] Mckinsey research has a similar message: only 11 percent of more than 500 executives polled around the globe strongly agreed with the statement that their leadership development initiatives achieve and sustain the desired results.[4] And MIT Sloan Management Research found that only 12 percent of respondents strongly agree that their leaders have the right mindsets to lead them forward.[5] It's pretty apparent that organizations don't feel their leaders are equipped to lead into the unknown.

LEADERSHIP BURNOUT

Many of us tend to approach our work as if it were a relentless sprint to the NBA Finals or the National Championship game. We pour all our energy into achieving our goals, only to wake up the next day and dive headfirst into the grueling preseason training all over again. This way of operating is often glorified in our hustle-and-grind culture, worn as a badge of honor.

However, this relentless focus on "what's next" can lead to burnout, disengagement, and significant challenges for our mental well-being. In fact, some research indicates that CEOs, in particular, are highly susceptible to these issues. They experience depression, often as a byproduct of burnout, at a staggering rate of 40%, which is double that seen in the general population. This immense stress and pressure can take a heavy toll on their mental health.

If leaders aren't taking care of themselves, and simultaneously keeping their finger on the pulse, they aren't going to be able to keep their current people engaged, activate high performance, or attract top talent to be competitive in the marketplace. Despite these challenges, this moment is an incredible opportunity for companies that create a super compelling offer and value proposition, which can generate immediate impact and position them to thrive in the future. A new era of business requires a new set of leadership rules.

THE INTERNAL GAME

As we address these current challenges and prepare for a future we won't even recognize, it's crucial that leaders develop the internal skills that will drive external results. We have to ignite the purpose-driven, future-focused, mindfully aware, and heart-centered leader within. We must become leaders that our people can look at and say, "Yeah, I see the vision and trust that person to lead me through the unknown process to bring it to life." We have to become the leader that we would have wanted to work for. Like John Maxwell says, "People follow the leader first and the vision second."

My experience working with over fifty thousand Gen Zers and Millennials, who now make up close to 50 percent of the workforce, supports this theory. When most Gen Xers and Boomers think of these two generations, the words that come to mind are lazy, entitled, and impatient. But the truth is that Gen Zers and Millennials are just aware of their options. Some might view this as a challenge, but the data is clear on what they want, which actually creates an opportunity.

Today's war for talent is not just between companies. It's between companies and the myriad of other options there are on the table for people to make a career.

It's a hard question to ask. Why should someone work for you for $50,000 to $70,000 per year when they can make the same amount of money building a social media following that they can monetize, creating affiliate stores online, or starting their own business? Companies need to wake up to the fact that the barrier to entry to entrepreneurship has never been lower.

And, while my personal belief is that of all the people who think they are cut out for entrepreneurship are not, it does provide benefits these generations value, including workplace flexibility, autonomy, and an opportunity to take full ownership in something—all of which drive fulfillment in work.

Here's the opportunity: Gen Z and Millennials want their work to contribute to something bigger than themselves, be where they belong, and have a leader who can guide them on their personal and professional journey. If you can create a culture that provides those perks, you can set yourself up to win in the future marketplace. The question is this: Will leaders and organizations stay stuck in past paradigms, or will they level up for the future?

While I'm far from some guru, I'll make a promise to you. When you're done with this short read, you'll be equipped with some of the same mindsets, strategies, and exercises I've shared through keynotes, workshops, and coaching with individual contributors and leaders at Fortune 500 companies and leading industry associations. Some of these include the likes of IBM, AmFam, Cisco, Morgan Stanley, and SHRM. And when you activate these principles, you can set yourself up to inspire, impact and influence your people, your organization, and maybe even the world.

Let's dive in.

"

Purpose is not the sole pursuit of profits but the animating force for achieving them. Profits are in no way inconsistent with purpose — in fact, profits and purpose are inextricably linked."

— Larry Fink

Chapter 1
UNLEASH THE ENERGY
OF PURPOSE

During his summer at The University of Virginia, Malcolm Brogdon, the 2017 NBA Co-Rookie of the Year, came to Milwaukee to work out with Thrive3, the basketball training company I built out of my college apartment. He had an incredible work ethic. We worked on his individual skills for a couple of hours and left the gym drenched in sweat. I still remember the picture we took afterward. It looked like someone had sprayed us down with a garden hose. He was all about the work. Malcolm was one of the most focused and motivated players I had ever been around. There's even a story that the student manager at The University of Virginia developed tendonitis in both hands because he rebounded for him so much. Talk about putting in the work!

After the workout, we decided to shower and grab some food at Bel Air, a Mexican restaurant in downtown Milwaukee. This was early in his college career. He had missed his freshman year due to foot surgery. At that point, his future in basketball was pretty uncertain. Was he going to be able to overcome this injury and have a solid career at Virginia, or was this going to throw a wrench into his basketball dreams? I asked him, "Do you want to keep playing after you are done at Virginia?"

He looked me straight in the eyes and responded with a "yes" that was grounded in a sense of resolve, humility, and confidence. Malcolm shared a couple of stories about when he went to Africa for mission trips as a kid. When he was eleven, his parents took him and his brother on a three-week trip to Ghana instead of going on vacation. Instead of enjoying rides at Disney World, they worked in daycare and maternity centers. In the "off" time, Malcolm played barefoot soccer with the kids in the neighborhood and realized how fortunate his family was compared to most people. And he grew up in inner-city Atlanta. He told me, "Even at eleven years old, this ignited a fire inside me. To do something bigger and create change."

Then when he was fourteen, his grandparents took him on a mission trip to Malawi, where he said people were living in even more extreme poverty. In Malawi, young girls traded education for traveling miles to gather water on a path where they were worried about being eaten by wild animals. This is a way of life for some kids in Africa. The situation is so dire that a child dies every ninety seconds because of a water related disease. He couldn't stop thinking about this.

After sharing these stories, he looked at me again and said, "So that's my motivation to make it to the NBA." It wasn't about a shoe deal. It wasn't about becoming an All-Star or signing multi-million-dollar contracts for the sake of money. It was about using those contracts and relationship capital from the NBA to start a nonprofit that provides access to clean water for rural villages in Africa.

Fast forward to today. Not only has Malcolm been named NBA Rookie of the Year and turned in five near All Star level season performances, but he's also launched the Malcolm Brogdon Family Foundation to serve his mission. The one that he shared with me eight years ago, back when he was in college. Because he operated with purpose.

Despite what you see in the media, the NBA lifestyle can be grueling. The long road trips, the ice baths, the rehab, the time away from family. You have to endure a lot of adversity—just like in business. But often, the determining factor in our ability to stay focused, locked in, and perform at our highest level is maintaining our emotional connection to our purpose. It's also something people can rally around when adversity hits at an organizational level.

PURPOSE-DRIVEN PROFITS

Now, this doesn't mean that in order to be purpose-driven, we need to go out and start a nonprofit like Malcolm or work for a charity. Purpose can be infused into our work. We can use it as a vehicle to create impact beyond revenue.

Kirk Souder is a purpose-driven leadership coach who works with executives at major brands like Amazon, Google, and Mattel, where he helps them uncover their individual purpose and connect it to their work. This creates a synergistic effect that drives creativity, fulfillment, and revenue. A part of this work is facilitating workshops. And a few years ago, the Senior Vice President of Global Product Design at Barbie was in attendance at one of his events. At this time, she was conflicted about staying with Mattel or leaving her job to pursue a career helping the disenfranchised. But she discovered something in this workshop. She tapped into an idea to use her position at Barbie to serve. Instead of starting up her own nonprofit, she created an entirely new line of diverse dolls—the Fashionista line—of all shapes and sizes that young girls could aspire to. They no longer only had a blonde-haired, blue-eyed, physically perfect doll to look up to. Instead, the girls had an authentic role model—someone they could see themselves in. The Fashionista line went on to win the TIME Magazine Invention of the Year two times and added millions to their topline revenue. The research backs up Kirk's approach:

1. Ninety percent of global employees in purpose-driven companies are engaged (Korn Ferry, 2016)[6] vs. 21 percent of the global workforce who are engaged (Gallup, 2021).[7]

2. Purpose-driven companies have been shown to out perform the market 15:1.[8]

3. Purpose-driven leaders have employees who are 70 percent more satisfied, 56 percent more engaged, and 100 percent more likely to stay with the organization (Harvard Business Review, 2014).[9]

As leaders, uncovering your individual purpose—and how it connects to the organization's purpose is the first step. It might even be a collaborative process with your entire senior leadership team to redefine this for the organization. You can do this by finding the commonalities of each individual's purpose to collectively define the path forward for the organization in the new world. Regardless, this north star is crucial to navigating the inevitable adversity as a leader or organization challenging the status quo. Research shows having a clearly defined purpose improves focus, resilience, and motivation—all qualities leaders need to navigate change.[10]

But the hard part is this. We have to model it. Only then can we help our people uncover their individual purpose. That's how we lead self-driven people who will take ownership of their work.

People don't want to be motivated. They want to be inspired.

When leaders live their purpose, that's exactly what they do. Inspire. This is how you tap into the power of intrinsic motivation that drives organizational excellence.

WHAT BEFORE WHY

Talking about purpose can often feel overwhelming. It's this big esoteric concept. The reality is that we have to reach people where they are. What drives them might not yet be a contribution to something bigger than themselves. When you look at it from the perspective of Maslow's hierarchy of needs, you can see that people might just be trying to meet their basic needs.

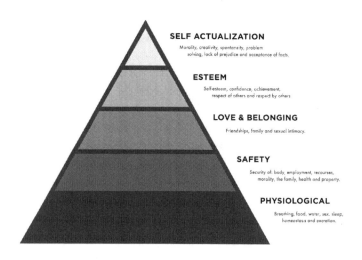

For some people, it might be the "what" before the "why." It might be just following their interests even if they don't make sense at the time. And that's totally ok. We are trying to uncover *what inspires people and gives people energy.*

Here are a couple of examples of the *What* before the *Why.*

The Architect

A friend of mine, Duane Jourdeans, used to be a high school basketball coach. He made it a priority to develop relationships with kids that went beyond the basketball court. He wanted to understand what drove kids so he could make an impact that lasted after their playing days were done. In his individual player meetings, he'd ask kids what they dreamed about. One year, he had a kid who dreamed of becoming an architect. Duane found an opportunity to make a connection. In basketball, a common drill to improve players' conditioning is to run what are called "lines." There are several variations, but essentially, players run from one side of the court to the other. When they reach the other sideline, they have to either touch the line with their hand or foot and sprint back in the other direction. When this player missed touching a line, Duane used it as an opportunity to connect this player's current work to his dreams. He'd say to him, "Billy, if you want to design buildings, you gotta be able to pay attention to details. How are you going to pay attention to all the details in designing buildings if you can't touch a line on a basketball court?" Duane could only speak to Billy this way because he invested in the relationship first.

Best Buy

Best Buy is an example from the business world that also emphasizes the what before the why. Hubert Joly, the former CEO of Best Buy who led their turnaround in the early 2010s, shares a story in his book *The Heart of Business* that brings the power of purpose to life. Part of Best Buy's turnaround strategy was a significant emphasis on their managers spending time with their front-line employees to understand their purpose. At one of their stores, there was a "blue shirt," as Best Buy calls its front-line employees, who dreamed of owning her own apartment. The store manager sat down with her and took the time to figure out what position she'd need to be promoted to in order to make her dream a reality.

They reverse-engineered this process by clarifying the skills this employee would need to develop to receive this promotion. The store manager stayed with her every step of the way, helping her develop her skills and earn a promotion. Someone who connects their work as a vehicle to achieve their dreams will inevitably be more engaged.

Questions are a great way to help people unpack and get to clarity:

- What do you dream about?

- What drives you?

- What problem would make your life better if you could solve it?

- What did you love to do as a child before adults told you to "be realistic"?

- How did doing what you loved as a child make you feel?

The more clarity you can uncover on what drives someone, the less you have to manage as a leader. Why? Because when someone is pulled by a dream, they have more intrinsic motivation and take more ownership in their work, which drives engagement. PwC research shows that highly engaged employees are 87 percent less likely to leave their roles.[11] Having a leader who invests in your life both in and out of the business is so rare that it cannot help but drive retention.

LEGACY EXERCISE

If we want to go deeper into purpose, we can leverage the power of legacy. It's just like your personal brand. You will have one whether you are aware of it or not, but if you're intentional about it, you can craft it. One way to get clarity on this is to start with the end in mind first and reverse engineer it. When I work with leaders in our coaching program or workshops, I have them write out their eulogies. I was introduced to this practice through reading one of Robin Sharma's books in my mid-20s. One thing that surprises most people is that even when they do this exercise in the context of business leadership, none of the insights have to do with driving more revenue and growth. It's about influence and impact. This might feel uncomfortable, but you and I both know that's exactly where we grow.

This exercise has massive potential to help you get clarity on what you want and how you show up in the world.

When we can figure out what we want people to say about us when we're gone, we can figure out how we want to live and lead every day.

And that becomes your legacy. The power of legacy is not what you get ten, twenty, or thirty years from now. The power is that it creates purpose in each moment. Here's how we can activate it.

Eulogy Instructions

1. Gather a couple of sheets of paper or your journal and a pen.

2. Set a timer for fifteen minutes.

3. Write out the eulogy that you would give about yourself.

Writing Prompts For Activating Legacy

- How did you love?

- How did you impact?

- How did you matter?

- What drove you?

- What problems did you solve?

- What did you instill in people?

- What adversity have you overcome that you've taught others to overcome?

This exercise is not usually a one-time thing. Instead, you can revisit and revise it as you continue to grow.

Because as you grow, so will your capacity to operate with deeper purpose and leave a legacy.

PURPOSE-DRIVEN VISION

Activating purpose happens at both the individual and organizational levels. Purpose at both levels is powerful on its own. But the magic happens when they are synergistic. When people understand their "why," they are more focused, more motivated, and take more ownership of their work. In short, they are more engaged. When organizations understand their "why" and communicate that purpose beyond some generic mission statement, it creates the north star that people can unite around. And, as we'll see in the next chapter, when purpose is clear, it creates a foundation to be future-focused.

"

Even though you may not feel or look the part now, you must envision yourself in your ideal state, activating your personal power and living in alignment with your stand and purpose. I learned in the SEALs that there's no such thing as perfection, only perfect effort. Through practicing a 'perfect' version of ourselves mentally, we'll slowly become that person in real life."

— Mark Divine

Chapter 2
THE FUTURE-FOCUSED LEADER

Staying future-focused is a trait of all leaders taking their people on a journey into the future. This is about combining two things — vision and optimism.

To lead people through change, we must emotionally connect them to a purpose-driven vision greater than their current circumstances—individually and collectively.

This is why starting with purpose matters. We must tell a story about why this future is worth pursuing and include them in the journey. Then we can tap into the emotional power of vision.

VISION

In 2006, I pulled my car into the parking lot of a junior college in Wisconsin for one of the first tryout sessions for the Wisconsin Playmakers. I started the youth basketball club for one reason: to provide kids with big dreams the skills, resources, and experiences for their dreams to come to life.

When I got out of my car, I was immediately approached by one of our coaches, who couldn't wait to tell me about a kid he had invited to tryouts that he had seen play in a game the day before. As I walked into the gym, I saw a sixth-grade kid grab a ball out of this blue canvas bag. He started to dribble the basketball. But not like a sixth grader. He dribbled like a college player who had worked countless hours to reach that level. He just had the ball on a string, snapping it back and forth. That caught my attention immediately, but later in tryouts, I noticed another thing about him. It had nothing to do with his skill level but his level of focus. Whatever we were doing, he was always there. His attention and energy were laser-focused at the moment. His eyes were locked on me because he wanted to soak up everything he could from this opportunity.

In 2006, Matt Thomas was just a kid with a dream. But, in 2019, he fulfilled his childhood dream of playing in the National Basketball Association by signing a $4.2 million deal with the Toronto Raptors. He played a contributing role for the Toronto Raptors in his rookie season, shooting close to 50 percent from the three-point line, and is now in his fourth NBA season. But this dream did not come true without tons of adversity.

When Matt was eleven years old, just a few months before I met him, his dad, who was battling drug and alcohol addiction, died by suicide. Then after Matt's sophomore year in high school, a friend's dad, who stepped in to be a father figure in his life, drowned in a boating accident.

During the summer after his sophomore year at Iowa State University, where he was on a scholarship, Matt had a couple of drinks at a party and decided to drive home. But the taillight was out on the car. He got pulled over and was arrested for a DUI. This would have been tough to deal with in and of itself, but he was also dealing with the fact that his late father had been an alcoholic. At this time in his life, he was trying to figure out who he was and his relationship with his dad. So he spent the night in jail thinking, "Am I an addict too?"

After he finished his career at Iowa State, he had an opportunity to play for the Los Angeles Lakers in NBA Summer League. In the Summer League Finals Championship, he scored 23 points, went 5-5 from the three-point line, and the Lakers won the title. He was on a high, thinking he would get an NBA contract. But no guaranteed offers came through, and Matt went to play in Spain for a couple of years before the Raptors offered him the opportunity to fulfill his childhood dream.

Matt had tapped into the power of vision. He woke up every day and decided that in some way, shape, or form, he would do something to work on his body, mind, or skills. To move closer to his dreams.

Matt taught me that having a vision greater than our current circumstances can pull us through massive adversity. We can use this vision to reverse engineer our process. Then we can weigh our choices against this vision every day. Are the choices I'm making today in alignment with the vision I have for my life, my job, my career, the people I'm leading, and what type of leader I want to be?

Even though this is an individual story, it applies at the individual and organizational levels. Purpose and passion (the what and the why) should drive vision. With the complexities of global organizations, it might be challenging for people to tie their day-to-day to the organization's mission. This is why it's crucial as leaders to spend time with your people on their vision for both their personal and professional lives. Working for leaders who care about their vision drives engagement, supports retention, and creates an employee experience that attracts top talent.

Part of attracting top talent is creating an experience so good that people can't wait to talk about it. If your people aren't recruiting for you, that means there is more work to do.

One way to do this is to support the human connection experience that goes beyond the numbers. Then we have to pursue this vision with optimism.

OPTIMISM

When I was a redshirt sophomore on our college basketball team, I was slotted in pre-season to be the starting point guard on a team that would be top 25 in the country in our division. I had put in a significant amount of work in the off-season and was excited about the upcoming season. I spent a ton of time working on The Gun, which is a basketball training device. This machine is positioned under the hoop, collects the shots in a net, and automatically passes the ball back to you, so you don't have to chase after your own ball. I spent so much time on the machine I got the nickname "Gunner." But, as pre-season started, I quickly found myself going from the starting point guard to the second team to the scout team, all within a matter of weeks. Needless to say, I was devastated—especially at a time when I tied all of my self-worth to my performance on the court.

I found myself sitting in my assistant coach's office, discussing everything that was going on. Soon, he asked me the proverbial question. "Mike, I have to know. Do you see the glass half-full or glass half empty?" I knew what he wanted me to say. But I'm a pretty candid person, so I looked at him and said quietly, "The glass... the glass is half-empty." He got out of his chair, pounded his hand on the desk, walked past me, and slammed the door shut behind him. Now, at that time, the truth wasn't that I saw the glass as half-empty. The truth was I felt like the glass had fallen off the table and shattered, and water was everywhere.

A few years later, I started my coaching career and was determined to be a much better coach than a player. I read everything I could on coaching and leadership—from John Maxwell to John Wooden. One book that significantly impacted me was *Success is a Choice* by Rick Pitino. A chapter in the book is titled "Being Positive Is A Discipline." It makes the case that positivity is not something that happens. It's not something we're born with. It's something that we choose. However, I like to replace "positivity" with "optimism" because I think positivity has so many negative connotations—for example, toxic positivity. What I've learned is that Coach Pitino is 100 percent correct. Optimism is a choice we make in each moment. Are we choosing to focus on the problems, or are we choosing to focus on the solutions?

There are no neutral thoughts. There is no in-between. We either have limiting beliefs that keep us stuck in the past or empowering beliefs that move us toward our vision.

In the context of the workforce, we leaders must ask ourselves if we see The Great Resignation as a problem or if we can reframe it as The Great Opportunity.

THE PERFECT DAY

One way you can approach defining your purpose-driven vision is to write out your Perfect Day. Ask yourself, "What would it look like if I worked with a Hollywood creative team with a multi-million dollar budget to create a movie of my purpose-driven vision?"

Write down the answers to that question on paper. I

find it very beneficial to write this out as a stream-of-consciousness story. We are prewired to connect to stories, and writing them helps make them real in our minds. In stream-of-consciousness writing, we don't let the pen come off the paper and write for an allotted time. This writing style shuts off our analytical mind and allows things to come through from our subconscious that might get blocked by our self-judgment of what we really want. It removes the thoughts that typically stop us, like, "That's stupid, we could never build that," or, "I'm not good enough to do that," or, "I don't deserve that." This is not about figuring out the how; it's painting the picture of the what.

We often block the possibility of the what because we are so focused on the how.

The Perfect Day Instructions

1. Grab a couple of sheets of paper or your journal and a pen.

2. Set a timer for fifteen minutes.

3. Write out your perfect day as if you were telling a story. "When I wake up in the morning ... "

Writing Prompts For The Perfect Day

- What feelings would you experience?

- What activities would you do that give you energy?

- What is the transformation you'd see in your people?

- What does it look like to bridge the gap from where your stakeholders are at to the dream of their future?

MOVING FROM THE "WHAT" AND THE "WHY" TO THE "WHO"

Being future-focused is about combining purpose, vision, and optimism to lock in on a future greater than our current circumstances. Part of developing a team or culture that attracts, retains, and engages is about getting clarity on the why and the what. The other piece is the "who." Who do we have to become to bring that purpose-driven, future-focused vision to life? One skill that is becoming increasingly important for leaders is mindfulness because it helps develop the emotional intelligence skills to lead ourselves and others.

" *Life does deal us a set of cards in the beginning that we cannot change, but we get to make our own decisions about how we are going to respond to life; mindfulness moves us from an automatic reaction to a thoughtful response."*

— Clif Smith

Chapter 3
UNLOCK THE POWER OF MINDFULNESS

It was March 2015, a cold, rainy spring day in Seattle. I traveled to the city to watch a player I had coached since he was thirteen years old play in the NCAA tournament. Instead, I found myself trapped inside my hotel room, sweating through my sheets, chronically nauseous, and having these crazy out-of-body experiences. I had my little mini goldendoodle curled up next to me in bed as

I experienced symptoms that were way worse than the flu. And, at rock bottom, I found myself curled up on the bathroom floor, vacillating between throwing up to passing back out in a fetal position. I felt like an addict. I could not figure out what was wrong with me. Finally, by the end of the weekend, it hit me. I was going through withdrawal, just like an addict. But not from heroin, oxy, or alcohol. I was going through withdrawal from a medication I had started taking fourteen years prior to help me battle depression. Before I moved out to Los Angeles, I lived in Wisconsin and would get incredibly depressed during the winters. I'm talking about a not getting out of bed until 3 or 4 pm level of depression. It finally reached a point where I could not take another Wisconsin winter and moved to Los Angeles purely for the weather.

A month after I moved, it was January and sunny something completely foreign to me. The big thing was that I felt way better than I had ever felt and decided to taper off this antidepressant medication that I had been on for fourteen years. But getting off this medication threw my brain and body into a state of chronic emotional instability. I'd go from laughing to crying to chronic anxiety to debilitating depression, all within a couple of hours. Board-certified doctors at UCLA have compared getting off the medication I was on to someone withdrawing from heroin. That's how bad it was.

A few years later, I learned that I was also dealing with Complex Post Traumatic Stress Disorder (C-PTSD) from previous experiences in my life. The emotional instability created by the medication withdrawal on top of C-PTSD prevented me from fully showing up in my business. A business that had grown year after year for a decade became incredibly volatile overnight, which only compounded the stress. When the only career you've known is a business you built out of your college apartment, there is no such thing as paid medical leave. I felt like I was in survival mode. Consciously I knew I wasn't, but trauma lives in our brain structure, subconscious mind, and body.

One of the most challenging parts about this was I just could not access the present moment. And, if I wasn't focused on the present moment, I couldn't do any of the work I wanted to do in the world. I knew I needed a tool to help me win this battleground that had been created in my mind. Because that's what it felt like every single day. I felt like I was going to war in my mind.

I don't share this story to give medical advice. The complexities of that are far beyond my scope of expertise. This was a personal decision that I made. Rather, I share the story to demonstrate the power of mindfulness. Because I did commit to a daily mindfulness practice. And after a couple of months of consistent practice, I realized why visionary CEOs like Steve Jobs, elite athletes like Kobe Bryant, and luminaries like Oprah all had attributed a form of meditation to their success.

MINDFULNESS: AN OVERVIEW

Since mindfulness has permeated pop culture, I think it's a good idea to give it some context. There is a lot of confusion around mindfulness right now, given how popular it has become. I even walked into Target the other day and saw a graphic t-shirt with the words "Gratitude, Kindness, and Mindfulness" stacked on it. I define mindfulness as "The ability to create the non-judgmental awareness of our thoughts, feelings, and actions in the present moment." Meditation is simply an exercise to train this higher level of awareness. As former EY Americas Mindfulness Leader Clif Smith says, "There's no bells, no beads, and no Buddha."

In no way, shape, or form am I trying to convince you to change your religious beliefs, give up all your belongings, and meditate in a cave in India for the rest of your life. Mindfulness is actually about being more engaged with your life. More engaged with your work. Mindfulness is a completely secular practice and has been proven in thousands of scientific studies to be a cutting-edge tool to train your attention, awareness, and focus. It's why NBA players, NFL players, and military branches implement mindfulness training.

The Science
Mindfulness meditation is to your brain what exercise is to your body. When you go on a strength training program, your muscles break down and grow back stronger. You can see the physical evidence of change in your body. When you engage in a mindfulness meditation practice, areas of your brain also change. There is an area in the front of

your brain called the neocortex responsible for focus, self-awareness, and decision-making. This area has actually been proven to grow in fMRI scans. Another area proven to grow is the temporoparietal junction, which is associated with empathy and compassion.[12] There's also an area at the base of our brain called the amygdala, which is responsible for our fight, flight, or freeze response. This area can actually shrink, making you less reactive to stress. And when we're less reactive to stress, we're more focused on the task at hand. We're less likely to be pulled out of a phone call, conversation, or email we're writing by the distractions and disruptions in our environment.

The Power of the Present

There are myriad benefits to practicing mindfulness, but for our purposes, we're going to focus on the power of the present moment. Research shows that many of us are only present about 50 percent of the day.[13] That means if we "work" forty hours per week, we only do intentional work for twenty hours. We spend time in the past stuck in guilt, shame, anger, or regret. Or we're in the future in anxiety, fear, or worry.

But the best thing you can do for your future self, the future of your organization, and the people you lead is to be fully in the present moment.

This is an exercise I sometimes take the audience through in a keynote or workshop to demonstrate the power of the present. You're going to go through each question one by one. The answer to each question is either the past, the future, or the present. While it might seem trivial, it paints the picture that all the states we value and want to operate in are derived from the present moment.

1. Where does anxiety exist?

2. Where does worry exist?

3. Where does uncertainty exist?

4. Where does regret exist?

5. Where does guilt exist?

6. Where does empathy exist?

7. Where does connection exist?

8. Where does a state of flow or being in the zone exist?

9. Where does high performance exist?

The states that we value as high-performing leaders all exist in the present moment. Marc Bertolini, the CEO of Aetna Insurance and mindfulness advocate, sums up the power of these questions. While participating on a panel at the Wisdom 2.0 Conference, he said, "I know I'm heading into a chaotic world...I'm going to be challenged about my own worth...unless I can bring myself to that environment in a steady and mindful way and be present in the moment in every opportunity I can, I can't help the people around me and lead them."

Aetna also proved being more mindful and present is good for the bottom line. From their internal study based on participants of their mindfulness program, they learned that they saved $3,000 on healthcare costs and gained $2,000 in productivity per employee.[14] *With an estimated 11-1 ROI, they added a total of $5,000 per employee to their bottom line.*

MINDFUL LEADERSHIP

Now, let's get a little more specific on how mindfulness can help level up our leadership skills in this era of work.

We Get What We Model

Number one is modeling. When we operate with more mindfulness, we create awareness of the behaviors, skills, and energy we are modeling for those we lead.

There's a direct correlation between how we show up and what is transferred to our people.

Leaders lose trust, connection, and engagement with the people we lead when there is a disconnect between how we show up and our expectations of how we want our people to show up. We're going to get from our people what we model.

One of my mentors started coaching the Marshfield High School boys' basketball team for summer leagues and tournaments. He would run some practices for them and always offered to train them outside of practice, "Whenever you want. As long as I don't have something going on with my family, I'll be there." On a hot, muggy, midwestern summer night in July at 1 am, Dave's phone rang. It was one of the high school players from the Marshfield team.

"Coach, can we get a workout in?" one of the kids asked, as Dave heard a couple of the others trying not to laugh in the background.

"Yep, I'll be there in fifteen minutes. You better be there."

He hung up. Fifteen minutes later, he was working out two players just like it was 1:15 pm, not the middle of the night. Brad Fischer was there, now the University of Wisconsin-Oshkosh Women's Head Coach, and remembers how much that night influenced his coaching career. "The music was turned up; players were sweating, and Dave coaching us up. He was trying to motivate us to be the best possible version of ourselves. He kept saying, 'No one else is working out right now.'" We have to model who we want our people to become. That's exactly what Dave did that night.

Managing Our Emotional State

The second way mindfulness improves leadership is self-management. With mindfulness, we can create awareness of and manage our emotional state. In today's talent marketplace, employees have the upper hand. So many organizations are struggling with retention, and a big part of that is the relationship your people have with those that lead them. No one wants to work for a leader that doesn't operate with self-awareness and can't manage their mental and emotional state. Have you ever made a bad decision on the fly, under pressure, not because you didn't have the skills or knowledge to make the right decision, but because of your emotional state? I have. I remember that when coaching one of my first basketball teams, I was incredibly hard on them after losing a game, and it took time and energy to rebuild the relationship and their morale. Afterward, I realized it was not at all what they needed at the moment.

Amateur leaders are driven by emotion. Mindful leaders are driven by intention.

Managing our emotional state helps us tap into the power of the Decision Gap.

The Power of the Decision Gap

As leaders, we make decisions all day long. And the decisions we make consistently add up over the long run and create the future of our lives, our people's lives, and our companies. This is why high performing leaders must be aware of the Decision Gap. The Decision Gap is the term I coined that refers to the mental space between what happens and our response. We decide what we fill this gap with. Do we fill it with worry? Do we fill it with a reaction? Do we fill it with anger? Or do we allow space for a pause and clarity to emerge? The more stress and velocity we deal with, the more the decision gap compresses. But the more mindfulness we have, the more awareness we operate with, the more that decision gap expands. Sometimes we don't see things clearly until we look outside ourselves— when we create separation between stimulus and response. We see things for what they are, not what our past experiences tell us they are. And that's what mindfulness gives us the power to do.

So many times, when adversity hits, we get caught in the storm. We become our emotions. But with mindfulness, we can:

1. Create awareness of the stressor or trigger
2. Detach emotionally
3. Get objective

Then, instead of becoming the storm, we are simply the observer of the storm. That's how we can step back into our power. From this place, we can make decisions aligned with our vision and values. When we operate from this place of integrity, we instill trust in the people we lead.

THE FOUNDATION IS SELF-AWARENESS

Now, if we want to put this into practice, we must develop self-awareness. Without self-awareness, we can't emotionally detach, be objective, and access the myriad other benefits of mindfulness. When we sit in meditation, we are forced to be with our minds and bodies. Out of that experience, awareness and insights arise. We also bring that sustained awareness out of the meditation session and turn it into actionable items. Why is this so important?

Awareness is the first step to transformation. If we aren't aware, we can't change. And if we don't change, we can't improve. Awareness is key.

I know what you're thinking: "I'm already self-aware." Maybe you are. But the research shows that of the 95 percent of people who think they are self-aware, only 10-15 percent actually are.[15] And, even if you are, there is always another level that you can get to. So how do we practice? Learning mindfulness is like learning how to swim. You can read a book about it, watch a video on YouTube or have someone explain it to you. But you won't know what it's like until you jump in the water. You can use hundreds of mindfulness exercises, but we'll cover four simple ones you can start practicing to hone this skill.

Mindfulness Meditation

If mindfulness is the skill, then meditation is the practice to develop it. Think of it like this: If you are an athlete who wants to improve their speed, you're going to spend time in the weight room, field, or court performing specific exercises to train this skill.

Mindfulness is no different. We have to spend

time training our minds to create the skill of self-awareness. Meditation is one exercise. In my experience, this is one of the hardest things to practice unless you have an audible guide. So we created one for you inside our Masterclass that provides several other resources not included in the book. You can access it at www.mindshiftlabs.com/masterclass.

Myths, Limiting Beliefs, and Challenges

Before we even get into the actual practice, I think it's super important to clear up some myths and challenges with starting a practice. I wish someone had told me these when I started because it would have changed my expectations of the practice and, therefore, my experience.

1. *I'm not being productive.*

When I first started meditating, this was my biggest challenge. It was a constant battle. While I knew the practice was good for me, I also felt I should be getting more things done.

What I learned, though, is that meditation doesn't take time. It gives you time.

When we bring mindfulness into our work, we operate with more awareness, intention, and purpose—all of which are tied to high performance.

2. Being proactive instead of reactive.

When I first started, I was what we call a "crisis meditator." I would meditate in reaction to a stressful event in my day. I'd use it as a tool to bring myself back to being centered. While that can be helpful, it's not the most effective. What's most effective is setting up your day with meditation to bring more mindfulness to the challenges that appear. As a high performing leader with more demands on your time than most, you know what gets scheduled gets done. Scheduling meditation into your day, even if it's for five minutes, will help build the compounding effects of the practice.

The "First Thing in the Morning" Myth

Almost all meditation teachers will tell you that the best time to practice meditation is at the very beginning of your day, as soon as you wake up. While that might work for some, you must be aware of what works best for you. I learned it might be best to practice after getting a workout in, especially for beginners. The physiological response from a workout creates a brain state optimal for meditation. Even Andy Puddicumbe, the co-founder of Headspace, one of the world's first meditation apps, starts his morning out with rowing before getting to his meditation practice. The key is to know yourself and what works best for you.

The Instant Zen Myth

Most people think that if they don't achieve an instant state of "Zen," they are not practicing right or are "not good at meditation." The truth is that until you become a master, you won't have that experience. When you first start (and even if you're almost a decade in like me), you are going to experience thoughts, feelings, and sensations arise. Even though they might be incredibly uncomfortable, that is totally normal. The longer your practice, though, the more space you will have between thoughts.

You have to shift your expectation from relaxation to training your mind to operate in more optimal states throughout the day. Relaxation might be a fringe benefit, but it's not the goal.

The goal is not to sit for ten minutes in deep peace and serenity. It's to take your meditation practice off your chair and out into the world so you can access more self-awareness, intentional action, and empathy that makes you a transformational, high-performing leader who wants to inspire, impact, and influence your people and the world.

In the following sections, we'll review guidance and instructions for starting and sustaining your meditation practice.

Posture and Room

You want to start by finding a distraction-free environment where you can dedicate ten minutes to this practice. Sit in a position where you are relaxed but alert. Sit as if a string is attached to the top of your head, pulling you up toward the ceiling. If that creates too much tension in your body, focus more on finding a position where you are relaxed. You can rest your hands on your thighs or fold them in your lap.

By no means do you need to sit cross-legged like a Buddhist monk in a monastery in India. The key is to be relaxed but alert at the same time.

Focal Points

Once you find this position, you'll focus on three focal points for a few minutes each before moving on to the next one. Any time your mind drifts, just catch yourself and bring your attention back to the focal point. Just think of that like a repetition in the gym.

Every time you catch yourself and refocus is a repetition. That's where you are strengthening your self-awareness.

1. Hear

The first one is going to be an audible focus. One of the best ways to cultivate mindfulness and break the pattern of incessant thinking is to focus your attention on your audible experience. This is why certain music can be very meditative. In your practice, you might hear a fan, cars outside, or someone walking in the hallway. Don't resist the sounds or judge them as good or bad. Just be aware of them. You can integrate all of the noises in your environment into your meditation experience.

2. Feel

The second is your body. You're going to use your felt senses to help center your mind. You can start at the top of your head and scan down through your toes. In this practice, you don't need to change anything you feel or relax. Simply be aware of what you feel as you scan down. You might feel something tight, sore, or tense. You might even feel the emotion in part of your body. A feeling in your body is almost always tied to a thought you are having or a deeply ingrained belief about something.

Awareness of what you are feeling in your body is a communication tool and bridge to your mind.

Being aware of your body is a great way to create more emotional awareness. Your attention drifting as you scan down is normal. Just return your attention to the top of your head and start again.

3. See
The last part is to just focus on your breath. This is not a conscious breathing practice. This is focusing on the awareness of your breath as it naturally rises and falls. As you breathe in and out through your nose, just become the observer of your breath. And, like the previous two focal points, any time your mind wanders, try to catch yourself and bring your

attention back to your breath.

That's it. You just meditated!

OTHER MINDFULNESS PRACTICES

Take 10

You can do this simple exercise whenever you need to center yourself. You can do it at your desk, in your car, or while walking from one meeting to the next.You simply exhale and then focus on taking ten even deep breaths. I'm sure you've seen a basketball player at the free throw line or a kicker before a field goal take a breath. They do this to anchor themselves in the moment. Ironically, a lot of them do this incorrectly. They breathe in and then almost force the air out. Science shows that people want to breathe out at the same speed or slower than they inhale. That activates the parasympathetic nervous system, which is responsible for our relaxation.

When most people think of breathing, they think of the inhale and exhale, but there are four parts to this breath:

1. The inhale
2. The top (when you are filled with air)
3. The exhale
4. The bottom (when you've completely exhaled)

You can say "in" on the inhale and count "one" on the exhale. "In" on the inhale, "two" on the exhale," up to a count of ten. For most people, that's enough time to center yourself. If it's not, don't worry. It's a practice, and you need to trust the process.

Moving Meditation

My favorite form of moving meditation is vinyasa yoga. It is not for everyone, but it can be a powerful practice to ease you into meditation. The reality is that most of us are more comfortable with physical activity than dealing with what's going on in our minds. It's actually what I started about a year before I began meditating. If you find the right teachers who emphasize the breath, yoga can be a moving meditation practice. You can learn to breathe through difficult poses and take that skill off the mat. I'm a big advocate of yoga because similar changes happen in the brain as mindfulness meditation.[15] This might be the best place of entry to the practice for a high energy, high-performer who has trouble sitting still. It's also a great tool to help you find the stillness in the movement—the stillness in the chaos of each day.

Walking Meditation

Walking meditation is also a super simple way to practice mindfulness. You simply watch your breath as you go out for a walk. You can also focus on the sensation of your feet. The key is to not be on your phone, listening to music, or on a call. Be fully in the moment. Sometimes I will do this with the Insight Timer App, where a reminder bell goes off every two minutes over the course of a twenty-minute walk with my dog. This bell triggers my attention back to my breath.

The more speed, velocity, and change we experience in our world, the more we need skills like mindfulness to stay on top of our game. These four practices can provide a great foundation.

MAMBA MENTALITY

One person who exemplified the power of mindfulness was Kobe Bryant.

Kobe, an eighteen-time All-Star and five-time NBA Finals Champion, was a player I studied in the basketball world.

While he had a notorious work ethic and an incredibly high skill level, something else gave him an edge.

In April of 2012, I remember watching the Lakers playing the Charlotte Hornets. And Kobe could not buy a shot.

He was on the right wing three.

Miss.

He got into the paint for a pull-up.

Miss.

He crossed a guy over and got an open look. Miss.

At this point in the game, towards the end of the fourth quarter, Kobe was 2-20 from the field and

0-7 from the three-point line. But down by two, with twenty-two seconds left, he had the ball in his hands. On the left wing, in an isolation situation, Kobe made a move on his defender. He got him back on his heels, making sure he wouldn't go by him, and rose up over the top to hit a three-pointer to put the Lakers ahead and win the game.

One thing Kobe could do better than any player I saw was place his attention and energy in the present moment. He wasn't in the past thinking about the eighteen shots he had missed. He wasn't in the future worrying about missing a game-winning shot. He was completely locked in.

Now, to the casual observer, this might look like talent. That's definitely what they would tell you on SportsCenter! But the truth is that he trained his mind every day—just like his skills and body— through a daily mindfulness meditation practice.

Kobe was able to deal with the game's ebbs, flows, and emotions because he trained his mind that way.

He was able to play relaxed but alert at the same time. He was relaxed enough so defenders didn't speed him up. The external things didn't speed him up. But he was alert enough to make a play. Alert enough to make a decision when he saw an opportunity. That's how we want to operate in life and business. We don't want the external to speed us up. We want to stay alert enough to make our play when opportunities arise.

He had the confidence to manage his emotional state, block out distractions, and stay centered because that's how he trained his mind. It didn't happen by chance.

Even amidst chaos, uncertainty, disruption, and change on the court—just like leaders are facing right now—he had the awareness to anchor himself in the present. We can do this through our breath, just as we discussed in the previous section.

Because if we can find our breath, we can find the present moment. When we find that, we can find the place within us that's always at peace and rest. And that is our innermost strength.

Sometimes we equate inner peace with complacency and weakness. But stillness and peace amidst chaos, change, and disruption is the ultimate strength.

LEADING OURSELVES TO LEAD OTHERS

The more velocity, disruption, and distractions we deal with, the more we must keep pace with developing skills like mindfulness. Mindfulness creates the self-awareness to lead ourselves in an increasingly chaotic world. It also creates the social awareness to develop a human-centric, heart-centered leadership approach. Let's get to the last chapter, Lead From The Heart, which helps foster a culture of engagement, belonging, and well-being.

" *In the past, jobs were about muscles, now they're about brains, but in the future, they'll be about the heart."*

— Minouche Shafik

Chapter 4
LEAD FROM THE HEART

When I started my speaking career, I put together my demo video and sent it out to several speaker bureaus. Very few got back to me, but I'll never forget one of them who did. At the end of my demo, there was a clip from a talk where I mentioned the word "love." This individual responded in her email, "Did you just say love in your video?" I replied, "Yes, why?" This individual told me they'd seen so many speakers' careers get killed because the speaker used the word "love" in their talks, and if I ever wanted a career in this world, I should remove it immediately.

This was eye-opening to me. In the basketball world, I saw coaches who transformed players' lives because those players knew that the coach loved them. In my personal experience, I could reach, connect with, and challenge players to maximize their potential because they knew I loved them. When I catch up with most players I coached and still stay in contact with, they end our calls by telling me, "I love you, man." Love transforms relationships.

I'd invite you to think about the most transformative relationships you've ever experienced. Remove yourself from the conditioning of business school or your corporate environment. Weren't the relationships that transformed your life built upon a foundation of love?

These relationships start with cultivating a love for ourselves. Leading others from our hearts begins with leading ourselves from our hearts.

Our relationship with ourselves reflects on our relationship with the people we lead.

We can extend that to others when we operate with more kindness, empathy, and compassion toward ourselves.

We can't transfer to others what we don't feel for ourselves.

With so much uncertainty, change, and chaos in our world, it's easy to be overly critical and judge ourselves. That is why if we want to lead others from our hearts, we must start by practicing self-compassion—an antidote to stress and burnout. When we show up for ourselves, we can show up for others. And that's exactly what current employees and the talent marketplace expect from their leaders. A Forbes article published in September of 2021 even makes the case that empathy is the top leadership skill.[16] One reason is that empathy makes people feel like they belong, a top human capital issue businesses face today.[17] The lack of connection in our digital first world has people craving to belong to something bigger than themselves, which is a huge opportunity for companies and leaders to capitalize on.

We develop a sense of belonging from different levels of our organization:

1. **Organization:** Do I feel aligned with the organization's vision, values, and purpose?

2. **Team:** Do I feel a sense of connection with my team?

3. **Leader or Manager:** Do I feel my boss is not managing me but mentoring me to become the best version of myself?

Maybe it's a hard-wired survival response. An eighty year Harvard study of health and aging has shown that close relationships keep people happy throughout their lives. These relationships with family, friends, and community delay mental and physical decline.

These social ties are better predictors of happiness and longevity than social class, IQ, or genetics.[18] If you can create a workplace that cultivates belonging, you will drive high engagement and foster a culture that attracts and retains top talent. It starts with how we show up and what we model for those we lead.

Even four-time NFL MVP quarterback Aaron Rodgers, who comes from one of the most alpha oriented environments one can experience, agrees. On the Aubrey Marcus Podcast, he said, "The greatest gift I can give my teammates is to show up and be someone who can model unconditional love to them."

In this last section, we'll focus on exactly what Aaron Rodgers is talking about the heart-centered leader.

THE THREE Cs OF HEART-CENTERED LEADERSHIP

In college, I had the best summer job in the world. I ran a basketball camp in my hometown, where I made enough money to travel around the country and work summer basketball camps. I'd drive from Wisconsin to a little town called Honesdale, PA, right outside New York City, to work the Five-Star camp with some of the top coaches in the country. I had the audacity, at twenty-three years old, to call up the Syracuse men's basketball office right after they had just won the national championship, asking if I could come to watch their workouts. On that trip, one of their assistants spent three hours in his office with me, talking Xs and Os. At the time, I was just a kid who dreamed of coaching Division 1 college basketball, trying to soak up as much as possible. But, of all the NBA and D1 coaches who gave me a glimpse of their world, there was a high school coach named Dave MacArthur, from a small town in Wisconsin, who drove around this big red Dodge Ram pickup truck and had no social media following, that had the most impact.

I have a memory of him that I'll never forget. It was a super-hot, humid July day in Wisconsin, and Coach MacArthur was directing a session at the Prairie du Chien Perimeter Camp. I had known Dave at that time for close to six years. Even though he was the coach at a high school twenty miles away from where I grew up, he would work me out in the summers (against our state high school association rules!), coached a club team that I put together, and took me with him to other high school games to teach me about the game and build a relationship with me. He was the high school coach that I only wish I had.

Now, since I was a college player at the time, my main job at a lot of camps was to be a demonstrator. During this session, MacArthur was putting me through a two-ball dribbling drill where I was demonstrating in front of about a hundred high school kids. I started on one sideline of the court, facing the other. I was doing a drill where I had to dribble two basketballs toward the first volleyball line that intersects the court. At that volleyball line, I had to cross one basketball over in front and dribble the other ball behind my back. On the first trip of the drill, I remember that I lost the basketballs. I grabbed the balls and started back over. On the second trip, I didn't go as fast because I just lost the balls and wanted to make sure I made the correct demonstration in front of the kids. Then on the third trip back, I lost the balls again, one of them rolling off my foot into the crowd of high school kids I was supposed to be demonstrating for.

I remember MacArthur blowing the whistle, looking right at me, and saying, "You suck, Mike! I can't believe that you can't even do that drill. You gotta put more work in. You suck." And, you know what? I got really good at dribbling the basketball behind my back. But it wasn't because he told me I sucked in front of a hundred kids. It was because I knew that man loved me.

I would have done anything for him because he focused on the three C's.

1. Communicate
2. Connect
3. Challenge

Let's explore each one in more detail.

Communicate

It might sound so simple it doesn't matter, but a relationship is the first step to helping your people be their best. I saw a lot of basketball coaches in my days that weren't great with strategy but had an unbelievable ability to develop relationships with their players and instill confidence, which ultimately led to success. Cy Wakeman, a leadership expert and New York Times best-selling author, said recently on The MindShift Lab Podcast, "Rules without a relationship equal rebellion." I don't know if I've ever heard a truer statement about why communication is so important. The more you invest in the relationship, the more you instill trust and the less you need to manage.

Connect

Connection involves communication, but on a much deeper level. Get to know your people personally. And do it authentically. This is especially important with so many new hires in today's world. Find out what they are passionate about, the music they listen to, things they enjoy outside of work, or what their kids do. And then support them in some way. Just like in the basketball world, I've seen so many leaders get more out of their people simply because they knew they were cared about beyond the bottom line. Why? This creates psychological safety to take risks, try new things, and be creative, which is a premium in today's complex world. When we feel cared about, our stress levels are reduced, freeing energy to focus on the things that matter.

Challenge

Only when we communicate and connect can we get to this third step. This is the state of the relationship when you can challenge people to do more, become more, and achieve more. Why is this important? Right now, people are looking for psychological safety and belonging in their work. But when those needs are met, I fully believe that people will be looking for a place of work where they have the opportunity for self-actualization. We all have an innate, often unconscious desire to maximize our human potential. A Fortune 500 company recently hired me to work with their senior leaders on shifting their leadership focus from inclusion to belonging. And during our session, I challenged them to go beyond belonging to self-actualization.

Because when we work for a place that helps us maximize our human potential and feel cared about and supported on our journeys, we can't help but feel a sense of belonging.

Creating a culture of belonging is how you stay on the cutting edge of organizational development.

CREATING AN INFINITE CULTURE OF HEART-CENTERED LEADERSHIP

A few years after my formative experience with Coach MacArthur, I was coaching our seventh-grade team for the Wisconsin Playmakers, the youth basketball club I mentioned earlier. There was a kid on the team who was tall and had a good feel for the game, but I just could not get him to go as hard as I knew he had to in order to get to the next level. When mid-season hit and we had our individual player meetings, I knew I had to dig deeper with this kid.

As we sat down on two folding chairs in the corner of the gym, I asked him the question I now realize I should have asked as soon as I met him.

I asked, "Paul, why are you here? What are you hoping to get out of this experience?"

He responded, "I want to be a D1 college basketball player."

So I said to him, "Ok, Paul. From here on out, I'm going to start treating you like you're a D1 college basketball player. When I'm hard on you, when I'm challenging you—this isn't me against you. This is me with you holding you to the standards of excellence that I know it will take to bring these dreams of yours to life."

And, in that second, everything changed. We had issues, I made him do tons of pushups, and I kicked him out of practice, but it all came from my heart. Paul connected every challenge to his dreams. *He no longer saw a challenge as something I was doing to him. He saw it was something I was doing for him.* Paul Jesperson went on to play in three NCAA tournaments, hit a game-winning buzzer-beater in March Madness, and is now an assistant coach for the Atlanta Hawks in the NBA. And I have no doubt that Paul is leading from his heart with the guys he is working with, just like Coach MacArthur did for me.

That's why I call this the infinite culture of heart centered leadership. When you, as a leader, decide to show up first, you create a compounding effect that can infinitely impact the entire organization. When we all feel like we have each other's back, we build connection and trust. In the words of trauma expert Dr. Bruce Perry, "Positive relationships and connectedness have the power to counterbalance adversity." This builds individual and collective resilience to lead through change, disruption, and adversity.

As leaders, focusing on these 3 C's will help initiate, strengthen, and maximize the potential of a relationship to support retention, drive engagement, and level up productivity- -all things that will produce bottom and topline results and deliver you more fulfillment as a leader than you could ever imagine.

FIND THEIR HOT BUTTON

One of my mentors from the basketball world was a long-time NBA assistant coach named Bill Peterson, who taught me another thing about the power of deep connections with those we lead.

In 1999 the Dallas Mavericks hired him to develop two young players that would go on to be Hall of Famers—Dirk Nowitzki and Steve Nash. But in the 80s, before Peterson was coaching in the NBA, he was a college assistant coach at Louisiana Tech. While he was there, they had a promising young freshman who Bill thought had the potential to be a star. But this kid just didn't understand what it took to reach his potential.

So instead of just trying to push this player harder in practice, he asked around the team and campus about this kid. He was trying to find what he liked outside of basketball—what Coach Peterson called his "hot button." Eventually, he discovered that this player loved cars but was incredibly poor and had no money to get one. So he scraped together a few hundred dollars to buy an old car that they could fix together during the summer. At the end of the summer, this kid went from never having a car to driving one that he fixed up himself with Coach Peterson.

Coach Peterson found his "hot button," something to connect with him on and to show him he cared for him outside of basketball. He taught this kid how to put in the work on the basketball court by working on the car. And, after they put this car together, this kid would do anything Coach Peterson asked of him.

Coach Peterson's evaluation of this kid's potential was

right. This kid, Karl Malone, went on to be an NBA Hall of Famer because Coach Peterson found his hot button.

LETTERS OF APPRECIATION

We must put human-centric, heart-centered leadership into action within our organizations. The truth is that if someone modeled heart-centered leadership for us, it already exists within us. We just have to remember it, activate it, and embody it. We all have someone like Coach MacArthur who impacted our lives.

Maybe it's a parent, a coach, a teacher, or someone you work with. There is someone who has impacted your life and helped you to be in the position of reading these words. Someone who influenced you to do more, become more, and achieve more. And you wouldn't be here without them. One way to tap into what they did for you is to express your gratitude to them through a letter of appreciation.

Letters of Appreciation Instructions

1. Grab a couple of sheets of paper or blank cards, envelopes, and a pen.

2. Make a list of one or more mentors that impacted your life.

3. Write out a letter of appreciation keeping the following writing prompts in mind:

Writing Prompts

- What did they do for you?

- How did they influence you?

- Who were you able to become because of what they did for you?

- How did they make you feel?

- What beliefs did they instill in you?

While writing the letter in and of itself can be a powerful reflection experience, I highly encourage you to find their address and put the letter in the mail. I've done this exercise multiple times, sending these letters to at least ten people. The exercise floods you with a tremendous amount of gratitude.

Writing a letter of appreciation keeps the Infinite Culture of Heart-Centered Leadership in flow. This "culture" doesn't have to be within the context of your current company. But the letter-writing exercise serves as a reminder of how someone showed up for you. And, by expressing your gratitude for this, you're reminding yourself that you can also embody the traits of that leader. By writing out multiple letters to people who have influenced your life, you're empowering yourself with more experiences and skills. Then the next time you face a challenge, you can draw on the experiences of all the people who have impacted you. You can ask yourself, if I could pull the best traits from all of the leaders that have impacted me, how would they show up in this situation? Would they show up with more presence? With more kindness? With more thoughtfulness?

Would they challenge me in a way that makes me feel safe to take a risk or make a move that challenges the status quo?

When we remember what our mentors and role models modeled for us, we can embody it in our work. If someone modeled it for you, it's within you. Writing them a letter of appreciation is one way to activate these traits.

CREATING BELONGING
IN A VIRTUAL WORLD

Writing a letter of appreciation can go beyond the leader who impacted you. It is a phenomenal way to make someone feel recognized, seen, and heard in an age when so many of us feel isolated. Maybe it's recognizing someone for their work on a recent project, voicing their opinion during virtual meetings when they are normally quiet, or taking a "risk" outside of their comfort zone even if they "failed." We get what we reward. The more specific we are with the appreciation, the more it means.

Think about how you'd feel if you got a note that said:

"Thanks so much for your great work on the project. I really appreciate your time and energy."

Versus

"I just wanted to express my appreciation for your great work on the project. The depth of your research, the presence you showed up with at the meeting, and the attention to detail changed the game for the client. I'm so grateful to be able to work with you."

Creating a sense of belonging in a virtual world is one of the top priorities for organizations looking to drive engagement and retention.

HEART-CENTERED LEADERSHIP REFLECTIONS

It was my last year of college while finishing up my degree in psychology. Sitting in my organizational development class, I heard the words, "You get what you measure."

I immediately took it to heart and applied it to my basketball coaching journey. It created intention around every drill, move, and skill we taught, as well as intention in our business decisions. And it's something that has stuck with me as I've transitioned from the basketball world to working with high performing leaders.

As leaders, it's important to reflect and measure whether we are showing up truthfully and objectively. In doing so, we begin to understand where we are, where we want to be, and how to implement a process to close that gap. While feedback is necessary and effective, objective, detached reflection is where we can learn to fully trust ourselves as leaders.

We step into our power when we rely less on the external and more on our own intuition.

We can ask ourselves the following questions to help us put the principles from this book into action:

1. Am I staying connected to my purpose?

2. Am I staying future-focused?

3. Am I leading from the present moment?

4. Am I leading from my heart?

5. Am I being the leader I would have wanted to work for?

6. Am I being the parent I would have wanted as a kid?

7. Am I being the spouse/partner that I would want in a relationship?

Some of these questions are tough to answer. I do not always show up as the leader I would have wanted to work for. But great leaders are always growing through reflection. They know that they need to transform themselves to transform their business. When they stop growing, their business stops growing. And getting objective on where they currently stand is the first place to start.

Culture is a direct reflection of leadership.

Close
THE RESEARCH DOESN'T LIE

When I was playing college basketball, we'd watch a lot of game film to learn what we were doing well and what we could do better to make adjustments. Our head basketball coach would always point out mistakes by saying, "the video doesn't lie." It's the same with the research we discussed throughout this book. It definitely does not lie. The Great Resignation proves that the way we work is not working. Even if people return to the workforce for a paycheck, these underlying grievances will pose major challenges for companies looking to drive growth and innovation.

Gallup, Mckinsey, and Deloitte have shown that we're stressed out, burned out, and disengaged, which is no longer sustainable in this new world of work.

Where does this all start to change? Leadership. The state of our culture is a direct reflection of our leadership. People crave meaningful work, their workplace to have a sense of belonging, and a more human-centered, connected way of working. People want more empathetic, compassionate, and mindful leaders willing to invest in their human potential. If we can walk away with one thing from this book, it is this: the future of business leadership is more purpose-driven, human-centric, and heart-led than ever before.

Organizations must place emphasis on their leaders creating connection with the people they lead, even if that is only one other person. They have to help them uncover what drives them, what their purpose is, and what they dream about. They must be able to connect those things to a compelling vision for the future of the company that is making an impact in the world. Mindfulness is one avenue organizations can take to place their people's well-being at the top of the priority list. People need to be cared about beyond the bottom line. When that happens, people will flourish and drive business results. And belonging is a top down initiative that can be ignited through heart-centered leadership and have a compounding effect on the entire organization. It starts with how we show up and what we model for those we lead.

Organizations and leaders being purpose-driven, future-focused, mindfully aware, and heart-centered are the prerequisites to compete in the new world of work. When developed and deployed, these competencies elevate engagement, win the War for Talent and create a culture of belonging.

The more we become the more we can give.

THE ROAD TO THE FUTURE

Despite the challenges we've labeled as The Purpose Crisis, The Engagement Dilemma, The War For Talent, Outdated Leadership Styles, and Leadership Burnout this moment is an incredible opportunity to position yourself and your organization for the future. Five years from now, circumstances are guaranteed to change.

Impermanence is a fundamental truth of our existence. So the question is not what will change. The question is, who will I become?

High-performing leaders know that the rate of internal growth must meet or exceed the rate of external change.

As one of my mentors, Ryan Estis, says, "You have to disrupt yourself before the market disrupts you." That's how we always stay on the cutting edge. When we become who we need to be, we can walk into the unknown trusting ourselves fully that we have the skills to adapt, navigate change, and thrive no matter what shows up.

IT'S HAPPENING FOR YOU

Knowing what we want, what we stand for, and who we are allows us to shift our perspective toward the future. The goal becomes growth instead of outcomes. We trust that if we focus on who we need to become—just as much as what we need to do—the outcomes will take care of themselves. Then, when adversity hits, we have a choice. We can either view our challenges as happening to us or understand them as opportunities for growth. It's often the case that we look back on adversity with appreciation because of what it's inspired us to do, become, or achieve. Many of our greatest opportunities wouldn't have shown up if not for adversity.

It might seem ironic, but growth and adversity aren't mutually exclusive —In fact, they're interdependent.

There is tremendous power in finding gratitude for the adversity we encounter. We must trust that a greater future is waiting for us on the other side and lean into the adversity with a growth mindset.

Because the more we become, the more we can give.

And what you can give because of the adversity in your life—what you can teach, what you can create, and what you can build—might become your greatest gift to your family, your organization, and the world. That gift becomes your legacy.

Go out there and show up for each other. Sometimes we play small because we think that we don't matter. But the truth is that we matter far more than we think.

NEXT STEPS

I hope the stories, mindsets, and strategies in this book have made an impact on how you think about business in this new era. But, what I really hope is that you take action and apply them. If you're a bold, driven, and future-focused leader your ideal next step is to go through the exercises in this book. We can't get buy in from our people unless we lead ourselves first.

To make this easy for you we've created a Masterclass.

TURN INFORMATION INTO TRANSFORMATION

Inside this Masterclass you'll get access to:

 Writing exercises to drive home the New Rules

 PDFs with reflection exercises and checklists

 Guided meditation audio tracks to support learning and practice

 An Intro To Mindfulness video series containing extras not included in the book

Get Started:

www.mindshiftlabs.com/masterclass

— TRUSTED BY WORLD-LEADING BRANDS —

lululemon

SHRM

Morgan Stanley

wework

Extending The Impact
WHAT MOST PEOPLE DO NEXT

What most people do next is drop a note to hello@mindshiftlabs.com to see if we can help you, your team, or your organization bridge the gap from your current reality to your vision of the future. We can lend support through personalized coaching, customized keynotes, leadership retreats, and actionable workshops—both live and virtually. I look forward to continuing the conversation with you soon!

WHO WE WORK WITH

Our clients are high-performing, bold leaders who desire to influence those they lead and impact the world. They have the open-mindedness to constantly step out of their comfort zones, think differently, and challenge the status quo.

WHAT WE DO

We help organizations level up their performance through non-traditional approaches to improving employee engagement, retention, talent attraction, and mindful leadership, ultimately impacting their ability to drive innovation, foster creativity, and solve the complex, critical challenges we face today.

HOW WE DO IT

We affect change at the root level—the individual. We empower them with sports performance psychology skills, mindsets, and strategies, blended with mindfulness and emotional intelligence, to unlock the human potential within. We believe that transforming people transforms organizations.

ABOUT THE AUTHOR

Mike Lee possesses a tremendous background spending time on the basketball court with elite NBA stars such as MVP's Steph Curry and Joel Embiid. He now shares relatable stories, actionable strategies and timely lessons from these experiences that transcend industries to help individuals develop purpose-driven, mindfully aware and heart-centered leadership skills.

His engaging, inspiring, and interactive programs at organizations like Morgan Stanley, AmFam, Cisco, SHRM and IBM have earned rave reviews from bold, driven, and future-focused leaders.

Drawing on the latest research from neuroscience, sports psychology, and personal experience, he's shared stories and practical exercises—across the United States, Europe, and Asia—to help people find their own inner power and poise to thrive in business and life.

Mike is also the author of the internationally sold book, UN/TRAIN and the host of The MindShift Lab.

ENDNOTES

[1] Dhingra, Naina, Andrew Samo, Bill Schaninger, and Matt Schrimper. "Help Your Employees Find Purpose—or Watch Them Leave." McKinsey & Company. McKinsey & Company, February 27, 2022. https://www.mckinsey.com/capabilities/people-and-organizational-performance/ourinsights/help-your-employees-find-purpose-or-watch-them-leave.

[2] Gallup, Inc. "State of the Global Workplace Report." Gallup.com. Gallup, September 23, 2022. https://www.gallup.com/workplace/349484/state-of-the-globalworkplace-2022-report.aspx.

[3] Tracy Brower, PhD. "Empathy Is the Most Important Leadership Skill According to Research." Forbes Magazine, November 9, 2022. https://www.forbes.com/sites/tracybrower/2021/09/19/empathy-is-the-mostimportant-leadership-skill-according-to-research/?sh=6b09bff13dc5.

[4] Feser, Claudio, Nicolai Nielsen, and Michael Rennie. "What's Missing in Leadership Development?" McKinsey & Company. McKinsey & Company, January 15, 2021. https://www.mckinsey.com/featured-insights/leadership/whats-missing-in-leadership-development.

[5] Walsh, Dylan. "What Makes Someone a Great Leader in the Digital Economy?" MIT Sloan, May 21, 2019. https://mitsloan.mit.edu/ideas-made-to-matter/whatmakes-someone-a-great-leader-digital-economy.

[6] Feldman, Janet. "Purpose Powered Success." Korn
Ferry. Korn Ferry, April 2, 2021. https://www.kornferry.
com/insights/this-week-in-leadership/purpose-powered-
success#:~:text=It%20turns%20out%20in%20a,rate%20
for%20the%20whole%20sector.

[7] Gallup, Inc. "State of the Global Workplace Report."
Gallup.com. Gallup, September 23, 2022. https://www.gallup.
com/workplace/349484/state-of-the-globalworkplace-2022-
report.aspx.

[8] McLeod, Lisa Earle. "Why Purpose Matters: Four
Business Reasons Plus One Emotional One." HuffPost.
HuffPost, April 8, 2012. https://www.huffpost.com/entry/
why-purpose-matters four_b_1257295.

[9] The Energy Project and Harvard Business Review.
"The Human Era at Work." Urban Land Institute. Accessed
November 30, 2022. https://uli.org/wp-content/uploads/ULI-
Documents/The-Human-Era-at-Work.pdf.

[10] Schaefer, Stacey M, Jennifer Morozink Boylan, Carien
M van Reekum, Regina C Lapate, Catherine J Norris, Carol
D Ryff, and Richard J Davidson. "Purpose in Life Predicts
Better Emotional Recovery from Negative Stimuli." PloS
one. U.S. National Library of Medicine, November 13, 2013.
https://www.ncbi.nlm.nih.gov/pmc/articles/PMC3827458/.

[11] PricewaterhouseCoopers. "Social Responsibility: Our Commit-ment to the Community." PwC. Accessed November 30, 2022. https://www.pwc.com/us/en/about-us/corporate-responsibility.html.

[12] Hölzel, Britta K, James Carmody, Mark Vangel, Christina Congleton, Sita M Yerramsetti, Tim Gard, and Sara W Lazar. "Mindfulness Practice Leads to Increases in Regional Brain Gray Matter Density." Psychiatry Research. U.S. National Library of Medicine, January 30, 2011. https://www.ncbi.nlm.nih.gov/pmc/articles/PMC3004979/.

[13] Escalante, Alison. "New Science: Why Our Brains Spend 50% of the Time Mind-Wandering." Forbes. Forbes Magazine, November 9, 2022. https://www.forbes.com/sites/alisonescalante/2021/01/28/new-science-why-ourbrains-spend-50-of-the-time-mind-wandering/?sh=328b2ac64854.

[14] Gelles, David. "At Aetna, a C.E.O.'s Management by Mantra." The New York Times. The New York Times, February 27, 2015. https://www.nytimes.com/2015/03/01/business/at-aetna-a-ceos-management-by-mantra.html.

[15] Kauflin, Jeff. "Only 15% of People Are Self-Aware -- Here's How to Change." Forbes. Forbes Magazine, June 29, 2021. https://www.forbes.com/sites/jeffkauflin/2017/05/10/only-15-of-people-are-self-aware-heres-howto-change/?sh=534bd32b8c21.

[16] Streeter, Chris C, Theodore H Whitfield, Liz Owen, Tasha Rein, Surya K Karri, Aleksandra Yakhkind, Ruth Perlmutter, et al. "Effects of Yoga Versus Walking on Mood, Anxiety, and Brain GABA Levels: A Randomized Controlled Mrs Study." Journal of Alternative and Complementary Medicine (New York, N.Y.). U.S. National Library of Medicine, November 2010. https://www.ncbi.nlm.nih.gov/pmc/articles/PMC3111147/.

[17] Tracy Brower, PhD. "Empathy Is the Most Important Leadership Skill According to Research." Forbes. Forbes Magazine, November 9, 2022. https://www.forbes.com/sites/tracybrower/2021/09/19/empathy-is-the-most-important-leadership-skill-according-to-research/?sh=c5a2a963dc5b.

[18] "Why Does Belonging Matter in the Workplace?" Deloitte United States. Accessed November 30, 2022. https://www2.deloitte.com/us/en/blog/human-capital-blog/2021/what-is-belonging-in-the-workplace.html.

WHERE HIGH-PERFORMING
LEADERS GO TO WIN
THE MOMENT

KEYNOTES AND WORKSHOPS

New Rules for the Future of Leadership
How the bold and driven can elevate engagement,
win the war for talent and create a culture of belonging

Unshakeable
Developing the resilient leader within

Game Changers
Counter-cultural performance principles that crossover
from the court to business and life

Mindfulness in the Modern World
How to beat burnout, elevate performance and cultivate
well-being in a volatile, complex and uncertain world

COACHING

The Upgrade
An inside out approach to elevating your
performance, people, and profits

"I love the storytelling!" — **IBM**

"So inspiring! The world needs to hear this!" — **SHRM**

Made in the USA
Columbia, SC
11 February 2025

53702131R00072